MOTORCYCLE RACING

RACING

The Fast Track

Supercross

JIM MEZZANOTTE

GARETH**STEVENS**

PUBLISHING
A Member of the WRC Media Family of Companies

Please visit our web site at: www.garethstevens.com
For a free color catalog describing Gareth Stevens Publishing's
list of high-quality books and multimedia programs, call
1-800-542-2595 (USA) or 1-800-387-3178 (Canada).
Gareth Stevens Publishing's fax: (414) 332-3567.

Library of Congress Cataloging-in-Publication Data

Mezzanotte, Jim.
    Supercross / by Jim Mezzanotte.
        p. cm. — (Motorcycle racing: The fast track)
    Includes bibliographical references and index.
    ISBN 0-8368-6425-5 (lib. bdg.)
    ISBN 0-8368-6574-X (softcover)
    1. Supercross—Juvenile literature. I. Title.
    GV1060.1455.M49   2006
    796.7'56—dc22   2005027217

This edition first published in 2006 by
Gareth Stevens Publishing
A Member of the WRC Media Family of Companies
330 West Olive Street, Suite 100
Milwaukee, WI 53212 USA

This edition copyright © 2006 by Gareth Stevens, Inc.

Editor: Leifa Butrick
Cover design and layout: Dave Kowalski
Art direction: Tammy West
Picture research: Diane Laska-Swanke

Technical Advisor: Kerry Graeber

Photo credits: Cover, © Brian J. Nelson; pp. 5, 7, 9, 11, 13, 15, 17, 19,
21 © Steve Bruhn

Printed in the United States of America

1 2 3 4 5 6 7 8 9 10 09 08 07 06

CONTENTS

Cover: Supercross has
a lot of high-flying action!

The World of Supercross

Have you ever been to a sports stadium? Maybe you watched a football or baseball game. But have you ever watched supercross?

Supercross is a kind of motorcycle racing. It is similar to **motocross**. Motocross riders race on outdoor dirt tracks. In the 1970s, some motocross riders began racing on tracks built inside stadiums. Supercross was born.

Today, the sport is a big hit. Many people watch it at stadiums. They watch it on television, too. Riders compete on small dirt tracks. They blast through tight turns and jump high in the air. Supercross is full of action!

Dirt always goes flying in supercross. It is an exciting and popular sport.

A Mountain of Dirt

A motocross track is laid out on hilly ground. It has mostly natural **obstacles**. A supercross track is built right in the stadium. Before a race, trucks haul dirt into the stadium. They bring in tons of dirt. Workers lay out many twisting turns. They also build all the obstacles. They build many bumps in a row, called "whoops." They build different jumps, too. A supercross track has a lot of jumps!

Supercross tracks are shorter than motocross tracks. They are narrower, too. Riders do not have much room to race. They go around very tight turns. During a race, fans can see the whole track. Thousands cheer for their favorite riders.

During a supercross race, riders often fly through the air. Their fans love to watch.

The Main Event

Many U.S. cities have supercross races. The races take place from December to May. AMA Pro Racing sets the rules for the races. It is part of the American Motorcyclist Association, or AMA. The races are mostly for **pros**. Only a few races are held for **amateurs**.

Riders first compete in races called **heats**. Then, they compete in the final race, called the **main event**. To race in the main event, they have to do well in a heat. Riders earn points for how they finish in a main event. First place gets the most points. At the end of the season, each rider's points are added up. The rider with the most points is the champ.

In supercross, riders first compete in heats. Only the fastest riders go on to the main event.

Flying High

Jumps are a big part of supercross. One kind of jump is the tabletop. It is a big rectangle of dirt. The jump is low but very long. Racers jump a long distance to get over it. Other jumps are higher. Riders may jump 50 feet (15 m) in the air — higher than a two-story building! Tracks often have two or three jumps in a row.

At the end of a race, riders sometimes do tricks. Jumping in the air, they may lie flat on their backs or let go of their bikes. Some riders compete in freestyle motocross. In freestyle, riders do not race. Instead, they earn points by doing tricks in mid-air. Freestyle is part of the Gravity Games and X Games.

Supercross star Jeremy McGrath (*left*) does a mid-air trick. Tricks like this one are a big hit with fans.

Built to Win

Supercross bikes have no headlights or horns. They cannot be ridden on regular roads. Their only job is to win races! The bikes are very strong. But they are lighter than other bikes, so they are easier to handle. Their engines are small, but they produce a lot of **horsepower** for their size.

A supercross bike has excellent **suspension**. The suspension connects the wheels to the bike. It helps the wheels move up and down over bumps. It keeps the bike steady on rough ground and helps the rider land after jumps. Special **knobby tires** dig into the dirt. Powerful brakes let the rider slow down quickly.

This supercross bike is light, strong, and fast. It is perfect for jumps and bumps!

13

Staying Safe

During supercross races, riders sometimes fall. They may even crash into each other. They can easily get hurt.

Riders need good protection. They wear strong helmets that cover the head and most of the face. They also wear goggles, to protect the eyes. Riders wear special clothing that is very tough. They wear plastic shields on their chests and pads on their knees and elbows. Their tall boots have metal in them to protect the toes.

Race officials also help with safety. If there is an accident, they will wave a yellow flag. All riders must slow down. Officials may even wave a red flag to stop the race.

Supercross racing can be tough on riders. They need protection for the head, face, and body.

Skills and Training

The top pros make supercross look easy, but it takes a lot of skill. Many pros began riding when they were young. They raced in amateur motocross. They spent hours practicing. As pros, they still practice a lot.

Pros have good balance. They react quickly to what happens around them. They know how to land from big jumps. They can find the fastest "line," or route, through a turn. They can twist the **throttle**, change gears, and apply the brakes — all at the same time.

It takes stength and **stamina** to race. Pros train all the time to stay in shape. They run and swim. They lift weights. They are some of the world's best-trained athletes.

A supercross race is hard work! To win, riders must stay in top shape.

Supercross Champs

Jeremy McGrath has been called the "King of Supercross." He was supercross champ seven times. As a kid, he competed in BMX, or bicycle motocross. He became famous for doing the **nac-nac** and other mid-air tricks.

Ricky Carmichael is famous for winning in motocross. He has won many supercross races, too. In 2001, 2002, 2003, and 2005, he was champ in both kinds of racing! Chad Reed is another supercross champ. He is from Australia.

James Stewart, Jr., is a new star. He turned pro in 2002, at age sixteen. Stewart has already been a champ in supercross and motocross. He is the first African American to be a champ in these sports.

James Stewart, Jr., is a young pro rider, but he has already won many races.

Let's Race!

Ready for the main event? You line up with the other riders. Fans are cheering and engines are revving. An official holds up a sign — thirty seconds to start. The **starting gate** falls to the ground. Everybody races to the first turn!

You scramble out of the turn, packed in with other riders. Then, you stand as you hit some whoops. A triple jump is ahead. You fly high above the ground. Then, you land, rear wheel first. In the next turn, you find the best line and pass a few riders. Only a few riders are ahead of you. You try to catch them. Your fans cheer you on!

A supercross rider wins the main event. Fans get to see all the action up close.

GLOSSARY

amateurs: in sports, people who compete without getting paid.

heats: in supercross, short races that decide who will compete in the main event.

horsepower: the amount of power an engine produces, based on how much work one horse can do.

knobby tires: tires that have large bumps, or knobs, for digging into the dirt.

main event: in supercross, the final race of a supercross event. Riders earn points for how they do in each main event of the season, and the rider with the most points becomes champ.

nac-nac: a mid-air trick in which a rider swings a leg over the rear wheel.

motocross: a kind of motorcycle racing that began in Europe after World War II. Supercross grew out of motocross and is similar to it. Motocross tracks are outdoors and have mostly natural obstacles.

obstacles: things that get in the way of going somewhere or doing something. On a supercross track, obstacles include different kinds of jumps and bumps.

pros: in sports, people who get paid to compete.

stamina: the ability to keep doing something.

starting gate: in supercross, a metal fence that flips down to the ground in front of riders, starting a race.

suspension: the system that lets a motorcycle's wheels move over bumps, so the rider stays steady while traveling on rough ground.

throttle: the part of a motorcycle that controls how much gas goes to the engine. Riders work the throttle by twisting one of the bike's handlebar grips.

FURTHER INFORMATION

Books

Dirt Bikes. Motorcycle Mania (series). David Armentrout (Rourke Publishing)

Jeremy McGrath: Images of a Supercross Champion. Ken Faught (Motorbooks International)

Supercross Racing. Dirt Bikes (series). Tim O'Shei (Capstone Press)

Ricky Carmichael: Motocross Champion. Michael Martin (Capstone Press)

Videos

The 5 Coolest Things: Supercross (Image Entertainment)

Fox Racing Presents Greatest Hits, Vol. 1 (Redline Entertainment)

Gravity Games: Summer Two (Vidmark/Trimark)

Terrafirma 7: Project MX (Red Distribution)

Web Sites

www.amamotocross.com
This web site is the official site for AMA supercross and motocross racing. It has information about both pro and amateur races and also has photos.

www.hondaredriders.com/motocross/landing.asp
Visit this site to learn about members of the Honda motocross team, including supercross star Jeremy McGrath. You can click on different riders for pictures and information

www.yamaha-racing.com/sx/
Visit this site to learn about the Yamaha supercross team, including supercross champ Chad Reed.

INDEX